LOUIE
the Bulldog

LOUIE
the Bulldog
VOLUME III

Louie Moves to the Country

BRENDA ZINTGRAFF
EDITED BY GINNY DONOVAN

XULON PRESS

Xulon Press
2301 Lucien Way #415
Maitland, FL 32751
407.339.4217
www.xulonpress.com

© 2020 by Brenda Zintgraff

All rights reserved solely by the author. The author guarantees all contents are original and do not infringe upon the legal rights of any other person or work. No part of this book may be reproduced in any form without the permission of the author. The views expressed in this book are not necessarily those of the publisher.

Printed in the United States of America.

ISBN-13: 978-1-5456-7046-0

Table of Contents

Chapter 1 The Country 1
Chapter 2 Bloody Paws 11
Chapter 3 Kittens, Kittens, Kittens 19
Chapter 4 The Old Horse, Cinnamon. 27
Chapter 5 We've Got Chickens 35
Chapter 6 Ranch Life 43
Chapter 7 The Fire Pit 51
Chapter 8 More of Louie. 59

Dedication

Volume III of the "Louie the Bulldog" series is dedicated to our dear Louie, who passed away peacefully in 2018.

Louie, you were a delight to our family for almost ten years. Your last days were extraordinary and you truly brought joy to everyone who met you. You loved to lay on the porch each morning while James and his dad drank their coffee. You were really "one of the guys." We loved how you spent the evenings with us watching the wide Texas sunsets. You lived a good life, Louie, and we really miss you. Rest in peace, old friend.

Chapter 1
The Country

After driving for what seemed like hours, the time had finally come. My family was moving to the country! My master, James, had talked about this move for a long time, and my heart was beating hard in my chest as the truck slowed down to pull into the property. We slowly approached a big black gate. Although I heard excitement in James' voice when he talked about moving to the country, the uncertainty of it all still worried me a bit. I didn't do well with change. But I chose to trust him just as I had trusted him in the past.

But I still felt jittery.

In the center of the gate was a large iron circle adorned with a giant bold "Z". As I looked out over the land behind the big gate, I could see a stone house in the distance. The country was much larger than I had realized! And it was beautiful.

As the big gate swung open wide for the truck to drive through, I felt a bit lost in these new surroundings. My master, James, entered through the gate with thanksgiving, but all

I could do was stare ahead silently; I did not understand the rejoicing in his heart. We drove about 200 yards down a driveway that seemed like it went on for an eternity. I could see James was beaming with a smile that looked like it stretched from one ear to the other. He drove slowly as he took it all in. Huge oak trees surrounded the house, and a perfect white wooden fence set the homestead off like a picture. Rose bushes hung over the white picket fence of the stone house, and I could see huge red barns further back behind the property.

"This is gonna be awesome, Louie!" James joyfully proclaimed.

I looked over at him with a blank stare, and then I looked back to the front window that showed nothing but strangeness ahead.

"What was my master *thinking*?" I wondered to myself. "We had a nice home with shade trees and a back patio at our old brick house. And where are the neighbors? The other houses are so far away in the distance."

I had learned to trust my master during our previous adventures, so I shuffled my feet back and forth and tried to wiggle my crooked tail to show a little bit of happiness. I felt pretty anxious, though, and being even a little bit happy was a challenge. However, despite my fear, I trusted that my master knew what he was doing and that surely this would be a good place to make a new home.

Across the road from our land, I could see cows behind a barbed wire fence. They all stood near the fence and stared at us as we drove by. I had never seen a cow before, and I sure hoped they were friendly like the bunnies

back at home. We drove very slowly down the rugged road.

Just then, a HUGE bunny darted across the road. He was faster than the little bunnies at home. And did I mention that he was ENORMOUS?

"Look, Louie, it's a jack-rabbit!" James exclaimed.

It was not your average bunny, like in my old backyard. It was gigantic! His ears astounded me as they stood taller than my whole body. My own little ears lifted high and my eyes were alert as I took in all the new things called "the country".

The truck came to a quick stop. James hopped out as soon as he could turn off the engine. He ran around to my side as I quickly and awkwardly jumped down to the graveled road and stood at his side.

"We are here!" James announced proudly. I could smell the cows immediately. And the cedar was popping with strong aromas. The land was so vast. I looked around and began to sniff everything. I had never seen such a big yard in my whole life.

"Come on, Louie, let's go explore this place," James said.

Wearing tall boots that protected him from snake bites, James began to walk quickly through the high grass. I had to hustle to stay beside him! Up ahead, I could see a pier on the edge of a beautiful pond. There were dragon flies hovering over the water and catfish popping the water's surface. It was like a picture in a book. After stepping off of the pier, we explored the pond's edge. I drank the water and waded in the shallow. I realized that I was starting to feel more peaceful as James and I explored the beauty of this new place.

By the time we got back to the stone house, I was so tired. There was so much to see and so much land that we had not even covered yet. I plopped down on the porch and panted hard. My master sat on a chair next to a table with a bottle of water and we just stared at the beauty of our new home in the country. James poured some water for me in a bowl, and I lapped it up quickly.

The cows in the next field were very interesting to me, and I watched them as they grazed. I wondered if they would mind me crossing the fence line and checking out their land at some point.

As we sat there cooling off in the shade, a huge moving truck pulled up to the house.

"It's here with all our stuff, Louie!" my master said with happiness in his voice.

The sound of the big moving truck was scary. It was so loud and heavy. I crouched down to get out of the way. The truck backed into the drive with a massive noise. The family members all began to pull in the driveway in their own vehicles and climb out with hands that were ready to help. They joined in to unload everything that was once at the old brick house in town.

I went inside to check out the stone house that would be our new living quarters. There was absolutely nothing in this home; no furniture, no pictures on the walls. It's scent was unlike anything I had smelled before. I wasn't so sure about this empty stone house. The kitchen was large with many cabinets that had nothing in them. A cold, lifeless fireplace was in the living room. Every room had a desolate feel. I had never been in a place like this before. The only word to describe what I saw was empty. It was lonely.

However, the family members poured in with great excitement and laughter.

I could hear them saying, "Oh, it's beautiful. It will be a perfect place for you."

However, I just wasn't sure about all this. I couldn't help but think of the bunnies I would miss back home and my backyard that I had faithfully guarded for years.

For hours, James and the family continued to bring boxes and furniture into the stone house. Lunch time came and everyone sat on the floor and ate pizza. It was a time of rest and laughter as the adults talked about how wonderful this new land would be. I ate pieces of left-over pizza and then plopped down on the front porch.

I wondered where my master and I would sleep tonight. This was a big country.

"I am sure he has a perfect spot for us," I reassured myself.

When evening came, James was tired from unloading of all the boxes. He threw an old quilt out on the grassy ground next to the house.

"Come on, Louie, we're gonna look at the stars tonight," he said.

I quickly trotted over to the blanket and plopped down. I took in a deep breath and blew out as I stretched my back feet out on the quilt. James propped his hands up behind his head for a pillow. We both laid there together as the darkness fell over us. One by one, the stars began to come out. I had never seen the sky so full of stars with a moon so bright. Thousands of stars were soon popping out all over the heavens. I had never seen so many stars before! My old neighborhood had no stars in the backyard. I could hear the crickets chirping and the locusts humming. There were coyotes howling in the distance. I lifted both ears as I listened to all these new sounds.

And that's when I noticed it: the country life actually felt pretty good! James and I laid there for hours just listening to the sounds until we fell asleep. I dreamed good dreams. My heart was finally glad to be here sharing such beauty with my master.

Chapter 2
Bloody Paws

The next morning, I awoke to the sounds of birds singing and cows mooing in the distance. My ears perked up as I lifted my head from the blanket. I remembered that I now lived in the country. The smell of the morning was different here. We had watched the stars the night before and there was a peace on this land called "the country". My heart was glad to be here sharing such beauty with my master.

I had been afraid to move to a new place before. But, it turned out that there was no need to be afraid. I knew better. My master was not afraid of anything; all I had to do was trust him knowing that if I just stayed close to him, things would go well.

"Hop up, Louie!" James said as he jumped to his feet. "It's a new day."

Like a bolt of lightning, I was up as quick as my master.

I stepped off of the old quilt and James shook the grass from it. James' dad walked out to the porch with large mugs of coffee. He headed for the porch where a bowl of dog food waited for me. I was hungry and gobbled it right up. James and his dad sat and visited about how wonderful it was to be in the country. I listened to them as they made plans for their new adventure. A large burp bellowed from my mouth. They both looked at me and smiled. Once again, I had pleased them.

"We need some cats for the barn, Dad." James said. "Cats will catch mice, too."

His dad smiled and added, "Now that we live on a ranch, we can also get some chickens and maybe a few horses."

"I would love to build a coop and then we could have fresh eggs" said James.

This was a whole new world for me, and I wasn't sure about all these ideas.

"We live on a ranch?" I thought. "A ranch in the country. Why do we have to get cats? And what are chickens?"

There was much to learn.

James' dad looked at me and said kindly, "Louie, we now live on a ranch and there is so much to do. But I promise that you're going to love it here."

That first week, we walked all over the ranch. I walked around the rock house and out to the barns and back with my master. It was a lot of walking. It seemed like twenty times a day we went out for a walk, and boy! I sure was tired by the end of each day.

We walked the fence lines and we walked through the fields. I waded through the ponds on the property. My master and I spent the next few days together as we just explored our new place.

One of the first things James wanted to do was to go fishing. We walked to the pier and I watched as he fished for catfish. One after another, James would catch a fish and then throw it back into the pond. Seemed strange for him to spend so much time getting a fish out of the water only to throw it back in. But it was fun.

James' dad bought a big red tractor and brought it out to the barn. Both James and his dad rode on the tractor daily and cut the tall grasses.

I was loving the outdoors, but the roads were very rugged. It seemed to be getting harder and harder for me to walk from the house to the

barn. I sometimes missed the soft grass that we had at our brick house in town.

After a few short days, my feet began to hurt so badly that I could no longer walk. I finally plopped down at the back door one afternoon and waited for James to come get me.

"What's the matter, Louie?" he questioned as he bent down to look at me closely.

There were drops of blood on the porch where I had walked. My paws were worn down from the country roads! James lifted my paws and saw that they were raw and bleeding.

My feet were too tender and were not used to rugged ranch walking. My delicate paws were only used for the indoors and soft, city grass. The gravel roads were beating up my paws to a bloody mess.

As soon as James examined my feet he said, "I need to call Dr. Gage."

James called the veterinarian immediately to get advice.

We were headed off to the veterinary clinic in no time. I was use to going to see Dr. Gage.

As soon as we arrived, I was hoisted up to the big silver table. Dr. Gage came right in to check me out.

"Your Old English Bulldog is a country dog now,' he said. 'He is going to have to build up some callouses for that country life," Dr. Gage told James. "But he will be fine in no time at all. Give it about a week."

After getting all the information we needed, James lifted me back into the truck. When we arrived home in the country, James quickly washed my feet and put ointment on my paws. Then he bandaged them with soft cloth for the night.

"You're gonna have to toughen up those paws, Louie," he said. "You're a country dog now."

Within a short few days, my paws began to heal. As they toughened up, hard calluses formed on the bottom of my feet. I was soon able to run and walk the gravel roads again. I had to take it easy as the callouses began to build on my paws. I had learned one of my first ranch lessons: bloody paws were not fun.

My master took good care of me and soon I was as good as new. The country life was a big adjustment for me, especially since I was an

Old English Bulldog who was growing up in Texas. But I soon learned to love the ranch, and I was ready to take on some new ranch responsibilities. I realized that in order to be a good Texas Bulldog, more than just my paws would need to toughen up.

Chapter 3
Kittens, Kittens, Kittens

The more time I spent on the ranch, the more the place grew on me. James and I went exploring each day, and that vet was right: my paws did toughen up. I could go anywhere with James now.

My life on the ranch was very happy. However, I was disappointed about one thing: James wanted a cat. He said we needed cats to keep the mice away from the barn. This made no sense to me whatsoever. I vividly remember that Pete, the old cat at our brick house in town, did absolutely nothing. Pete never chased mice. He just laid on the porch and slept. He didn't even like me. I wondered how James could possibly think that a cat could (and would!) catch a mouse.

It was a spring day when James surprised everyone with not one cat…but two small kittens. They were very young and crying loudly. One was a pure white kitten with long hair.

"I think I will call you Lily," James announced.

She purred loudly as James picked her up and held her over his head.

The other kitten was a Siamese. She was almost completely white with little black tips on her ears and nose. James named her Co-Co.

Both kittens were brought into the barn that would soon be their new home, and at first, they were afraid of me. I had no plans to hurt them. However, just like Pete, they both hissed at me each time I came near them.

Each day, James went out to the barn to feed and check on them. I wanted to see the new kittens, too, so I followed him. James held the kittens and loved on them as he did me when I first came to this new home. The kittens seemed to like the large barn and all the attention. As the days passed by, they didn't seem to mind that I was there, too. They played for hours and I usually laid on the barn floor and watched them. In a few months, both the kittens had grown into cats. They played outside

the barn and seemed to love their new life here, just like me.

It was the fall season and Co-Co and Lilly were both soon to have kittens. My master made boxes for the baby kittens to be born in; there was a box for Lilly and a box for Co-Co. The time was soon to come for Co-Co and Lily to have their young.

It was an exciting day when those kittens were all born at the same time! We had kittens everywhere. Co-Co had six kittens and Lily had four. We had ten new baby kittens. Those mama cats were amazing! I just had to watch from a distance because the mama cats were very protective of their babies. The kittens were so hungry and tiny meows came from all of them at the same time.

Co-Co had three Siamese kittens that looked just like her. She also had two black kittens and a calico. Lilly had two orange ones and two white ones that looked just like her. The two boxes were brimming with kittens. They could hardly move or even crawl. It reminded me of when I was a baby bulldog and had to stay in a box with my mama.

After a few weeks, the kittens were beginning to climb out of their boxes and crawl all over the barn. The mama cats couldn't keep them in the boxes any longer. They were all too curious to get out and explore their new world. I just laid down on the floor in the barn. The little kittens were not afraid of me. I found myself laying as still as I could while they climbed all around me. What a joy it was! They were so fun to watch as they played. I was so happy to have all these little friends; twelve cats all together.

Everyone that came over got excited about the kittens. James' nieces and nephews all came and each had a kitten to play with.

But then the unthinkable happened. Co-Co, the Siamese mama cat, got very sick and couldn't feed her kittens anymore. She began to hide away and left her babies crying. I felt sorry for her six kittens because they wanted warm milk to drink and Co-Co was too sick to take care of them. I knew they were going to die if something didn't happen quickly. Co-Co had no strength to take care of her kittens, and in a short time, she was gone. My heart was broken. All her kittens were left behind as orphans.

Lily could hear the kittens' cries. She knew that Co-Co had died. She went to Co-Co's box and one by one she carried each of Co-Co's babies over to her litter. She gently laid them in with her own babies and loved them. Then she laid down on her side and allowed all ten of the kittens to drink her milk. As the little kittens drank frantically, Lily licked each one as if they were all her own.

Lily was a hero. She saved the day. The kittens purred loudly as they drank milk. When they were all full, they fell asleep all snuggled up near their new mama. She licked each one and cleaned their faces after they ate. I was amazed. I had never seen such a hero in my whole life.

The kittens grew and became cuter by the day. They were all wonderful barn cats. The barns were surrounded by fields of coastal hay, and that's where the mice lived. Mama Lily began to teach the kittens how to catch tiny mice from the fields. Every day, the little kittens would stand back and watch as mama Lily would hunt for mice and catch her prey. Then she would give the little mouse to the kittens to play with. Soon, each kitten began to catch their own mouse. At first, it was a game. But after many catches, they became champion barn cats and they all served their purpose in keeping the mice out of the barns.

As I laid on the barn floor and watched the kittens, they played all around me and were never afraid of me. They never hissed at me or seemed to mind my presence. They just played as if it didn't matter that a big ole' bulldog was there. They were all becoming the little friends that I had once wanted.

Now I could understand the reason for getting cats. The country needed them. Everything in the country had its purpose.

I could see that now.

Chapter 4
The Old Horse, Cinnamon

Today was the day. I had watched the cows from a distance long enough. I was ready to go meet them and become their friend. I decided to cross our barbed wire fence and check out the cows in the neighbor's pasture. It was exciting to walk the land with my master, but today I was exploring new things, and I was doing my exploring alone.

On my own, all by myself, I planned to cross the barbed wire fence that separated our land from the neighbor's. The mama cows were having their babies and I wanted to see them up close. I slipped under the barbed wire and slowly walked up to the cows. Each of the mama cows didn't seem to mind me being there. They were all watching me closely but were not afraid of me. I found myself being accepted by the cows and it was fun. I loved the baby calves. They were so cute and curious. I watched them as they drank milk from their mamas. Each baby calf would jump and play and run around the pasture. I loved my new friends. I could smell them and walk with them and they didn't mind. I liked the way the cows smelled. The strong country air reminded me that I was a Texas bulldog. I was allowed to walk with the cows and their calves.

The feeling of being accepted was strong when I walked slowly with the herd. This was the life of a country dog, and there was so much joy to have so many friends. I was so happy that I crossed over to the next field and met those cows, too.

Several days went by as I continued to cross the old rusty barbed wire fence. James never knew that I was stepping off our property. I chose to go in the early morning before anyone was up. Each morning when I went outside, I found myself taking a stroll over to the neighbor's pasture, just to see the baby calves. I knew my master would not approve of me leaving our land. He thought it was too dangerous. But what would it hurt?

However, one particular morning, I noticed that two horses had been added to the pasture. One was a big brown quarter horse named Lightning. He was gentle and just ate grass all day. The other horse was an old Welch pony named Cinnamon.

"This should be fun," I thought. "New friends!"

Cinnamon was red with one white foot, and she was not friendly toward me at all. She was old and bossy and she didn't like the idea that I was crossing over into her territory.

Something inside my heart told me to keep my distance from her. I knew that I should not cross the line today. But my curiosity was too great. I wanted to see my little friends, so nothing was going to stop me.

What happened next I shall never forget as long as I live. I should have listened to that voice of warning inside of me. Cinnamon, the old red horse, had had quite enough of my friendly visits. When she saw me cross the fence, she looked at me with a fiery red in her eyes, lowered her head, and came running at me full speed. I tried to get out of the way. I stopped in my tracks as I heard Cinnamon whinny in a loud voice. I looked back and she kept running toward me. She was wild and furious. I tried to act calm. I hesitated as long as I could, but she would not stop. She bolted toward me and turned her hips as her heels kicked into the air. I felt the blow of that white hoof as she kicked me in the ribs. I couldn't get out of the way fast enough. My side burned as I went rolling across the pasture like a bowling ball. Cinnamon ran past me. I felt the punch from her hooves. I rolled over several times in the pasture. I scrambled to my feet to get out of the way but Cinnamon made

a wide turn to run me over again. I knew I was in serious trouble. I looked for the fence line as I scrambled to get up off the ground. You have never seen a bulldog run as quickly as I did that day. I couldn't scoot under the barbed wire fence fast enough. Cinnamon was right on my heels as I barely escaped.

"What just happened?" I wondered, trying to catch my breath. "Did that old horse really just kick me?"

I felt a burning sensation as I ran for home, and I felt fear as I ran back to the covered porch on our own land. I was in a state of shock. My master had been watching from the porch. He waited for me as I came running. It was a relief to see him with open arms.

"Louie, you are not supposed to cross the boundary of our property. You know better," James said as he embraced me.

I knew he was right. I knew it was not safe over there. But I wanted to walk with the cows and the baby calves. Danger was across the line and I had walked right into it. I had stepped over my safety zone, and it had scared me.

I hobbled over to the rose bushes and plopped down in exhaustion.

"Louie, you have a big ole' hoof print on your side!" James exclaimed. "You're lucky that old horse didn't trample you, boy."

I laid down to rest in the sun. My tongue was hanging out as I panted. I could feel my side pounding from the blow. This was a tough lesson to learn. The country life had a lot of new things for us. But horses were a whole different experience that I had not expected. From that point on, I kept my distance from Cinnamon. Never again would I cross over the barbed wire fence. I knew I would miss walking with

the cows. But watching them from a distance would be much safer.

Day after day, when Cinnamon was grazing, I would bark in a low voice to let her know I was there. She would look at me and stare. The look in her eyes continued to be wild and fiery. It was called a warning. I knew exactly what she was thinking, and that was, "I can run faster and kick harder than you, ole' bulldog!" She was right.

Cinnamon and I never really became friends. We just stared at each other through the old barbed wire fence.

Chapter 5
We've Got Chickens

Mornings were my favorite time of the day. James and his dad always rose at the crack of dawn, and they often had their coffee on the porch. Birds would sing at the top of their lungs, and the crisp morning air was wonderful. I would sit with everyone on the quiet porch and stare out over the land. The sun glistened down on the large pond in the front pasture, making the water shimmer with sparkles. This was a time when words were not needed. Silence brought rest and the rest brought peace. I could smell the steaming coffee in my master's cup as he sipped slowly.

James' dad was also a slow coffee sipper. After one such sip he looked over at James and said, "I am gonna get those baby chickens soon.

We need to build a chicken coop for them. Will you help me?"

I lifted my head and wondered what baby chickens were. This should be interesting.

"I would love to, Dad," James replied. "Chickens will bring us some fresh farm eggs."

"Well, I have all the supplies and we need to get started today," his dad responded.

So, after one more sip of coffee, both of them were off to start work on the chicken coop. I jumped up and followed right behind.

Over the next few weeks, I watched James and his dad as they gathered lumber, nails and all kinds of wire for what they called a "chicken coop". For days, they measured and sawed and hammered. I had never seen before seen or even been around chickens, but my master was excited about them and that made *me* excited. James and his dad built a large wooden frame and put chicken wire all around it. This was to protect the chickens from other animals that could harm them. Small wooden beds were made for the chickens and were comfortably lined with straw.

"This is where the chickens will lay their eggs," James patiently explained to me.

Everything was built to perfection and painted white. When the work was complete, they printed "THE COOP" over the door with black paint. It was a fine chicken coop. James and his dad took great pride in all the work they had done for these chickens.

"We are almost finished!" James exclaimed. "We just have to make an area for the babies to be safe and warm."

Inside the barn, a small spot was created for the baby chicks who would soon be delivered. It was also covered with chicken wire, and sand was spread across the bottom so the chicks could run about. A water dispenser and food feeder were placed at the back of the box. I watched intently each day as the chicken project came together.

The day finally came when the baby chicks arrived. There were about 24 baby chicks all chirping loudly. They were placed gently in the brooding pen. As each chick was put into the box, they ran around the pen frantically. They had fuzzy fur and were so cute. I wanted to play with them and smell them. I waddled back and forth in anticipation, greatly desiring to interact with these fuzzy cuties, but James only allowed me to watch from a distance.

James' dad checked on the baby chicks each morning. It was a daily routine to have coffee and give special food called "scratch" to the baby chicks. They grew very fast. It wasn't long before each chick soon grew feathers instead of fur. As they grew, they didn't fit in the little brooder any more, and they had to be transferred to the large chicken coop that had been so carefully built for them. Those little chickens had no idea how much work had gone into their perfect cage. Each chick was moved to the large pen and had lots of room to run. Their heads were constantly bobbing up and down as they chirped loudly. After a few weeks in the new coop, they were allowed out in the farm yard to explore. The chicks were excited to have an even larger place to walk and peck the ground. When evening came, James' dad rounded up the chicks to the coop again. Each chick seemed to know what to do. They came running to their safe place. It was a secure place for them to roost at night and eventually lay eggs.

Those chickens were funny, NOISY creatures. One was a rooster that was louder than any of the others. He crowed early in the mornings and every one could hear him. Even when I was asleep in my bed at the house, I could hear him crow.

The chickens were not afraid of me, but it was my job to keep the chickens off the patio. Each time they came too close, James would say, "Go get those chickens, Louie!" I jumped up and ran them off. They knew they could not come onto the patio. I had a big responsibility now. I could not touch the chickens, but I would not let them cross the patio line.

Rooster was a bit challenging. He didn't like the fact that I could tell him what to do.

The chickens brought lots of excitement to the ranch. They laid their eggs and James gathered them each day. Rooster crowed every single morning. He thought he had to do this to wake the countryside.

All these new animals added excitement to the ranch. I loved watching the daily chores, and most of the time, I just sat and observed. However, my daily walks to the pond and the barn remained my favorite form of exercise.

I truly believe that life in the country is the best thing that could have ever happened to me. When I first heard about moving to the country, I was afraid. But now all is well here.

An Old English Bulldog living happily in the country–who would have thought?

Chapter 6
Ranch Life

The Christmas season arrived once again. All the grandkids came out to the ranch to climb up in the loft of the barn and bring down the big red Christmas boxes. One by one, each box of decorations were gently brought to the floor of the barn. As strings of Christmas lights were strung out, laughter rose from the voices of the children.

"Hey, kids. Separate the glass balls from the nutcrackers," James said.

Everyone helped with the opening of the Christmas decor, and I watched as they untangled lights and separated each decoration carefully. All the breakable balls had a special box that had to be carried into the house for the tree.

Garland was stretched over the white picket fence to make a perfect scallop.

"I'm going to jump up on the big swing and get a better look," I thought. I loved sitting up high to see better.

So, I took a big jump to get out of the way. The view was much better from up there. I could see each grandchild as they separated the Christmas boxes on the patio.

James knew that I was curious but didn't want to get into trouble. Suddenly he got a funny idea as he grabbed some colorful lights and began to string them around me as if I were a Christmas tree. Then he laid a small nutcracker right next to me and took a picture. I had my red Christmas sweater on to keep warm. All the grandchildren laughed as he made me look ridiculous. I could tell that James was delighted in this little moment of pleasure.

"Oh, brother," I thought. "This is so humiliating."

But I just sat there and smiled to myself as everyone giggled. I knew it was all in fun.

"I must look like a chubby little Christmas tree," I thought.

The holiday season is a time for family and happiness. This was Christmas number nine for me. I watched year after year as the family grew older and became closer. I was always included. I am a very blessed dog.

A big red four–wheeler was the new Christmas gift for all the grandkids to ride. It was the wildest toy on the ranch, and I found myself utterly exhausted trying to keep up with it. I loved to chase the kids as they rode all over the land; I chased that four-wheeler until I could run no more. My efforts to catch the kids on the four-wheeler always ended in defeat, but I sure did have fun trying.

The holiday season was a joyous time with lots of family. As the Christmas season came and went, it was time to start preparing the land for the coming harvest.

In the large utility barn, there was a large Kawasaki Mule off-road vehicle, with a large bed in the back for farm equipment.

"Hop in, Louie," James exclaimed as he patted the bed of the vehicle. "Let's go for a ride!"

I jumped in as quickly as my short, chubby body could. I always loved to be with my master and go along for rides. I was allowed to ride in the back and go all over the land with him. We drove across the small creek bed that followed the tree line. A tall deer feeder was located there; we had to fill it each week. James used the Mule to load the corn for the feeder and to carry tools. We stopped and filled the feeder and then moved on to the next job. There were always fences to be mended. James and his dad worked hard to keep every fence sturdy. I watched as if it were my duty and responsibility to be there. So much work had to be done, and I felt important as they brought me along.

Cameras were placed along the fence posts to capture pictures of animals crossing the land. Although we never saw as many animals during the daytime, there were so many animals that came out at night! We saw photos of raccoons, coyotes, bobcats and all kinds of critters. They never knew that they were being caught on camera. The deer came in large groups to eat since they loved the corn we provided. Putting corn in the feeders was one of the most exciting things to do on the ranch!

The ranch life continued to be very busy. James' family bought a huge red tractor in order to move the big bales of hay for the animals. I watched from a distance as James' dad used it

to dig trenches and scoop dirt from the ponds to make room for more water sources.

The tractor was used for all the heavy work on the ranch. The grandkids came out and helped with clearing the brush along the tree line of the property. Then huge brush piles were made with the tractor; we would burn the piles on misty, windless days. It was a big work day when everyone came to help burn brush. All these things were required to keep the land looking good, and everyone had to pitch in to get the job done.

A huge lawn mower was used to trim all the grass and weeds around the farm house. I watched from the porch as James mowed. James' mom would bring lemonade and snacks as the jobs on the ranch took place because all of that hard work made everyone very hungry and thirsty!

Each morning, James' mom would go out to the chicken coop to gather eggs. I sat back and watched with amazement as the master-hunter cats continued to catch mice from the field. All of the ideas and plans for the ranch, from fresh eggs to mice-hunting cats, were falling into place!

Activity was always happening on the ranch. But even during the busiest seasons, it was a calm place. I never knew the country would be so entertaining…or so peaceful. There had been so much to learn. James and his family loved their ranch, and I loved it, too.

This place is a good place. I have learned over time that wherever my master is, there I want to be also. I am simply happy wherever he is.

I believe we are here to stay.

Chapter 7

The Fire Pit

Winter was bitterly cold on the ranch. Spring was coming soon and the wind howled across the fields of coastal hay. The land looked like golden hands waving in the wind. My eyes watered as the cold air hit my face. I turned to go back into the warm house. James had made a crackling fire in the stone fireplace to take the chill off. As I walked into the doorway, I slowly plopped my heavy body down on my soft bed. The hot fire felt good.

My body moved much slower now since I was much older. Nine years is an old bulldog. I found myself wanting to stay inside near a warm fire every day during the winter. Winter was not my favorite time of the year; it seems I became cold so easily. In fact, the cold weather made me miserable. I was ready for spring to come sooner than later.

I loved to sleep all the time. Whenever I slept, I could hear everyone laughing because of my loud snore. I knew they loved the sound, so I tried to snore even louder when I heard them laugh.

There is nothing like snuggling into my thick soft bed, my cold nose buried down into the warmth of my blankets. I mostly observed all of the ranch activities from a distance. I felt most comfortable staying in my bed, as my old age made me feel stiff. I slept for hours until I felt James come to check on me. He would put his gentle hand on my head. I could feel his love for me.

"Ole' Louie," my master said, as he patted my head. "Are you cold? Let's go for a walk. It will be good for us".

I jumped up to go, following wherever he went. The big barn protected us from the wind as we walked around the house and came to a wooden bench. We sat down and looked out over the land together, and I knew this was one of our quiet moments. This was always one of my favorite times: he didn't talk, but the silence brought peace. We just delighted in being together and seeing what the good Lord had blessed us with: this ranch, the country life, a home. Our time together had now become quality. This was a good season in our lives.

Suddenly James looked down at me and announced, "Louie, we need a fire pit."

I knew he had come up with an idea, but once again, I thought, "What's a fire pit?"

As he stared into space, he said, "We could poke the fire and cook hotdogs over it."

I could see a smile come over my master's face as his mind developed his new idea. I had learned to know my master just by watching him, and I now knew his heart. He always intended good things for us. I could tell that a new idea had just exploded inside of him, and if James had an idea, he would quickly turn his idea into a reality.

We returned to the warmth of the house, and James sat at the table and began to draw a plan for the fire pit. I curled up at his feet and looked up at his face; James made all kinds of facial expressions as he drew.

"This is gonna be awesome, Louie!" James said. "It won't be long now!"

A few days later, a crew of men arrived at the ranch to measure for the fire pit. The plans were in the making and a fire pit was about to be created! A huge twelve-foot circle of cement was poured for a foundation. The round pit was built with beautiful white stone. Then, four small stone benches were built around the fire pit for

guests. There was plenty of room for people to sit and enjoy a fire. A beautiful little bridge was also created to go over the water drainage ditch to the sidewalk. Everything was perfect. It took several weeks to create this special spot, but the day came when it was finally completed. James gathered wood and sticks to make our first fire in the pit. As I sat and watched the fire begin to burn, I could see the joy in my master's face. The red coals glowed as they created a crackling sound. James looked proud as he poked his fire. It was wonderful as we sat outside together and enjoyed the stars. The heat from the fire kept me from being too cold in the crisp night air, and I could hear James humming a song as he poked the fire with a long stick. We watched in silence as the fire crackled and popped. A fire pit was a good and relaxing thing for the ranch.

Almost every evening, we went to the fire pit for another night under the stars. Once, my master even brought marshmallows to roast on a stick. It was wonderful. And oh, were they good! I always got a taste when one was burnt black.

There is such peace on this ranch. As I sit and think about my life, I believe I would like to spend the rest of my days here. As far as I'm concerned, there is no better place on earth; here in the country by my master's side is by far the best life a dog could ask for.

I am an Old English bulldog–a very Old English bulldog. I love this life I've been given, and I want to spend the rest of my days right here under the stars of this big wide sky.

As I sit here with my master, I have a knowing inside, that I will spend the rest of my days here, in the country, on this peaceful ranch. We will never leave this place.

I have been given a good life. I thank God each day for my life and for such a good master. Counting my blessings is a very easy, for I am a very blessed dog.

Chapter 8
More of Louie

James, his dad, and Louie

Louie watching over the ranch

Having fun with James

Ranch Life

Lazy days on the patio

Two of the kittens on the wood pile

A drink of water

Trinity (one of the grandchildren and Louie)

The author, Brenda Zintgraff, and Louie

Lightning Source UK Ltd.
Milton Keynes UK
UKHW020718210220
359075UK00005B/60